Kaplan Publishing are constantly finding new ways to make a difference to your studies and our exciting online resources really do offer something different to students looking for exam success.

This book comes with free MyKaplan online resources so that you can study anytime, anywhere. **This free online resource is not sold separately and is included in the price of the book.**

Having purchased this book, you have access to the following online study materials:

CONTENT	AAT	
	Text	Kit
Electronic version of the book	✓	✓
Progress tests with instant answers	✓	
Mock assessments online	✓	✓
Material updates	✓	✓

How to access your online resources

Kaplan Financial students will already have a MyKaplan account and these extra resources will be available to you online. You do not need to register again, as this process was completed when you enrolled. If you are having problems accessing online materials, please ask your course administrator.

If you are not studying with Kaplan and did not purchase your book via a Kaplan website, to unlock your extra online resources please go to www.mykaplan.co.uk/addabook (even if you have set up an account and registered books previously). You will then need to enter the ISBN number (on the title page and back cover) and the unique pass key number contained in the scratch panel below to gain access. You will also be required to enter additional information during this process to set up or confirm your account details.

If you purchased through Kaplan Flexible Learning or via the Kaplan Publishing website you will automatically receive an e-mail invitation to MyKaplan. Please register your details using this email to gain access to your content. If you do not receive the e-mail or book content, please contact Kaplan Publishing.

Your Code and Information

This code can only be used once for the registration of one book online. This registration and your online content will expire when the final sittings for the examinations covered by this book have taken place. Please allow one hour from the time you submit your book details for us to process your request.

Please scratch the film to access your MyKaplan code.

Please be aware that this code is case-sensitive and you will need to include the dashes within the passcode, but not when entering the ISBN. For further technical support, please visit www.MyKaplan.co.uk

AAT

AQ2016

Final Accounts Preparation

EXAM KIT

This Exam Kit supports study for the following AAT qualifications:
AAT Advanced Diploma in Accounting – Level 3
AAT Advanced Certificate in Bookkeeping – Level 3
AAT Advanced Diploma in Accounting at SCQF Level 6

Kaplan Feedback
Tell us what you think

PUBLISHING

British Library Cataloguing-in-Publication Data

A catalogue record for this book is available from the British Library.

Published by:

Kaplan Publishing UK

Unit 2 The Business Centre

Molly Millar's Lane

Wokingham

Berkshire

RG41 2QZ

ISBN: 978-1-78740-006-1

© Kaplan Financial Limited, 2017

Printed and bound in Great Britain.

CONTENTS

Features in this exam kit

In addition to providing a wide ranging bank of real exam style questions, we have also included in this kit:

- unit-specific information and advice on exam technique

- our recommended approach to make your revision for this particular unit as effective as possible.

You will find a wealth of other resources to help you with your studies on the AAT website:

www.aat.org.uk/

Quality and accuracy are of the utmost importance to us so if you spot an error in any of our products, please send an email to mykaplanreporting@kaplan.com with full details, or follow the link to the feedback form in MyKaplan.

Our Quality Co-ordinator will work with our technical team to verify the error and take action to ensure it is corrected in future editions.

UNIT-SPECIFIC INFORMATION

THE EXAM

FORMAT OF THE ASSESSMENT

The assessment consists of five independent tasks and will be assessed by computer-based assessment.

The assessment will cover:

- the process of preparing financial statements and incomplete records
- producing final accounts for a sole trader
- understanding the accounting requirements for partnerships and preparing financial statements for partnerships.

Task types will include calculations, completion of ledger accounts, completion of pro-forma statements and multiple-choice or similar questions.

In any one assessment, students may not be assessed on all content, or on the full depth or breadth of a piece of content. The content assessed may change over time to ensure validity of assessment, but all assessment criteria will be tested over time.

The learning outcomes for this unit are as follows:

	Learning outcome	Weighting
1	Distinguish between the financial recording and reporting of different types	10%
2	Explain the need for final accounts and the accounting and ethical principles underlying their preparation	7%
3	Prepare accounting records from incomplete information	27%
4	Produce accounts for sole traders	31%
5	Produce accounts for partnerships	20%
6	Recognise the key differences between preparing accounts for a limited company and a sole trader	5%
	Total	**100%**

Time allowed

2 hours

PASS MARK

The pass mark for all AAT CBAs is 70%.

 Always keep your eye on the clock and make sure you attempt all questions!

DETAILED SYLLABUS

The detailed syllabus and study guide written by the AAT can be found at:

www.aat.org.uk/

INDEX TO QUESTIONS AND ANSWERS

This document references IFRS® Standards and IAS® Standards, which are authored by the International Accounting Standards Board (the Board), and published in the 2016 IFRS Standards Red Book.

EXAM TECHNIQUE

- **Do not skip any of the material** in the syllabus.

- **Read each question** *very* carefully.

- **Double-check your answer** before committing yourself to it.

- Answer **every** question – if you do not know an answer to a multiple choice question or true/false question, you don't lose anything by guessing. Think carefully before you **guess**.

- If you are answering a multiple-choice question, **eliminate first those answers that you know are wrong**. Then choose the most appropriate answer from those that are left.

- **Don't panic** if you realise you've answered a question incorrectly. Getting one question wrong will not mean the difference between passing and failing

Computer-based exams – tips

- Do not attempt a CBA until you have **completed all study material** relating to it.

- On the AAT website there is a CBA demonstration. It is **ESSENTIAL** that you attempt this before your real CBA. You will become familiar with how to move around the CBA screens and the way that questions are formatted, increasing your confidence and speed in the actual exam.

- Be sure you understand how to use the **software** before you start the exam. If in doubt, ask the assessment centre staff to explain it to you.

- Questions are **displayed on the screen** and answers are entered using keyboard and mouse. At the end of the exam, you are given a provisional result.

- In addition to the traditional multiple-choice question type, CBAs will also contain **other types of questions**, such as number entry questions, drag and drop, true/false, pick lists or drop down menus or hybrids of these.

- You need to be sure you **know how to answer questions** of this type before you sit the exam, through practice.

KAPLAN'S RECOMMENDED REVISION APPROACH

QUESTION PRACTICE IS THE KEY TO SUCCESS

Success in professional examinations relies upon you acquiring a firm grasp of the required knowledge at the tuition phase. In order to be able to do the questions, knowledge is essential.

However, the difference between success and failure often hinges on your exam technique on the day and making the most of the revision phase of your studies.

The **Kaplan Study Text** is the starting point, designed to provide the underpinning knowledge to tackle all questions. However, in the revision phase, poring over text books is not the answer.

Kaplan Pocket Notes are designed to help you quickly revise a topic area; however you then need to practise questions. There is a need to progress to exam style questions as soon as possible, and to tie your exam technique and technical knowledge together.

The importance of question practice cannot be over-emphasised.

The recommended approach below is designed by expert tutors in the field, in conjunction with their knowledge of the examiner and the specimen assessment.

You need to practise as many questions as possible in the time you have left.

OUR AIM

Our aim is to get you to the stage where you can attempt exam questions confidently, to time, in a closed book environment, with no supplementary help (i.e. to simulate the real examination experience).

Practising your exam technique is also vitally important for you to assess your progress and identify areas of weakness that may need more attention in the final run up to the examination.

In order to achieve this we recognise that initially you may feel the need to practice some questions with open book help.

Good exam technique is vital.

KAPLAN PUBLISHING

THE KAPLAN REVISION PLAN

Stage 1: Assess areas of strengths and weaknesses

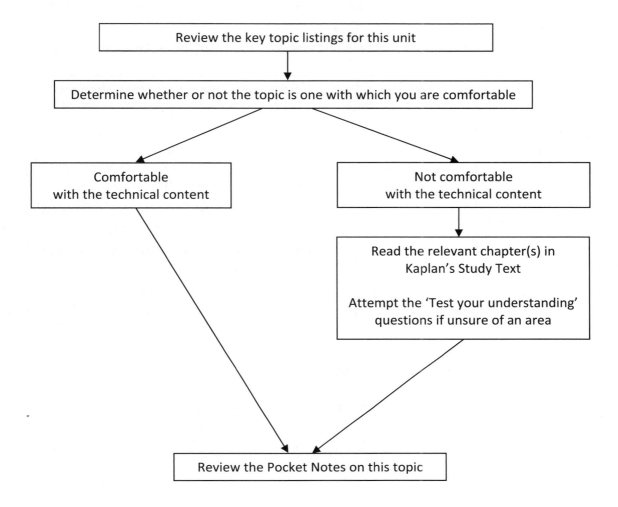

Stage 2: Practice questions

Follow the order of revision of topics as presented in this Kit and attempt the questions in the order suggested.

Try to avoid referring to Study Texts and your notes and the model answer until you have completed your attempt.

Review your attempt with the model answer and assess how much of the answer you achieved.

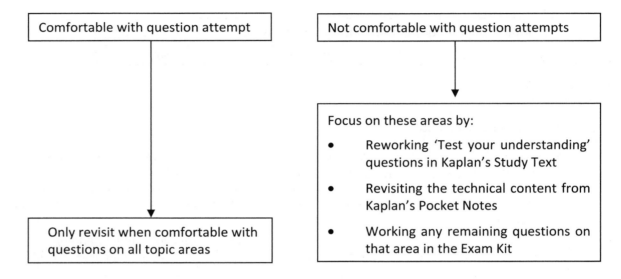

Stage 3: Final pre-exam revision

We recommend that you **attempt at least one mock examination** containing a set of previously unseen exam-standard questions.

Attempt the mock CBA online in timed, closed book conditions to simulate the real exam experience.

Section 1

PRACTICE QUESTIONS

INCOMPLETE RECORDS AND RECONSTRUCTION OF LEDGER ACCOUNTS

1   A CATERING BUSINESS

You are working on the financial statements of a catering business for the year ended 31 May 20X3. You have the following information:

Day book summaries:	Goods £	Sales tax £	Total £
Sales	241,000	48,200	289,200
Purchases	94,000	18,800	112,800

Balances as at:	31 May X2 £	31 May X3 £
Trade receivables	26,000	12,000
Trade payables	21,500	16,800

Further information:	Net £	Sales tax £	Total £
Office expenses	8,000	1,600	9,600
Office expenses are not included in the purchases day book			

Bank summary	Dr £		Cr £
Balance b/d	9,620	Travel expenses	14,000
Trade receivables	294,875	Office expenses	9,600
Interest received	102	Trade payables	115,150
Cash sales (inc sales tax)	18,000	HMRC for sales tax	27,525
		Drawings	101,000
		Payroll expenses	10,000
		Balance c/d	45,322
	322,597		322,597

(a) Using the figures given above, prepare the receivables (sales ledger) control account for the year ended 31 May 20X3. Show clearly discounts as the balancing figure.

Receivables (Sales ledger) control account

(b) Find the closing balance for sales tax (VAT) by preparing the sales tax control account for the year ended 31 May 20X3. Use the figures given above.

Note: The business is not charged sales tax on its travel expenses.

Sales tax control

		Balance b/d	4,300

2 LOCKE TRADING

You are working on the financial statements of Locke Trading for the year ended 30 September 20X9. You have the following information:

Day book summaries:	Goods £	Sales tax £	Total £
Sales	195,000	39,000	234,000
Purchases	93,600	18,720	112,320

Balances as at:	30 Sep X8 £	30 Sep X9 £
Trade receivables	16,500	20,625
Trade payables	8,700	12,130

Further information:	Net £	Sales tax £	Total £
Admin expenses	37,000	7,400	44,400
Admin expenses are not included in the purchases day book			

Bank summary	Dr £		Cr £
Balance b/d	8,725	Travel expenses	4,650
Trade receivables	225,000	Office expenses	7,800
Interest received	75	Trade payables	105,200
		Admin expenses	44,400
		Rent	1,500
		HMRC for sales tax	6,450
		Drawings	25,000
		Payroll expenses	13,600
		Balance c/d	25,200
	233,800		233,800

You have been advised that the trade receivables balances and trade payables balances at 30 September 20X9 are stated before accounting for a contra amount of £500 which has been offset against amounts due between Locke Trading and another business which makes both purchases and sales on credit to Locke Trading.

(a) **Using the figures given above, prepare the payables (purchase ledger) control account for the year ended 30 September 20X9. Show clearly discounts as the balancing figure.**

Payables (Purchase ledger) control account

(b) **Using the figures above find the closing balance for sales tax (VAT) by preparing the sales tax control account for the year ended 30 September 20X9.**

Sales tax control

		Balance b/d	2,300

3   FIRST POSITION BALLET SUPPLIES

You are working on the financial statements of a business called First Position Ballet Supplies for the year ended 31 December 20X2. You have the following information:

Day book summaries:	Goods £	Sales tax £	Total £
Sales	105,000	21,000	126,000
Purchases	92,000	18,400	110,400

Balances as at:	31 Dec X1 £	31 Dec X2 £
Trade receivables	8,100	11,500
Trade payables	12,400	9,800
Prepayment	300	450
Accrual	250	?

Returns day book summaries:	Net £	Sales tax £	Total £
Sales	19,000	3,800	22,800
Purchases	8,000	1,600	9,600

Bank summary	Dr £		Cr £
Balance b/d	23,400	Electricity expense	5,000
Trade receivables	96,590	Trade payables	?
Interest received	3,810	HMRC	6,100
		Rent	10,000
		Balance c/d	4,200
	123,800		123,800

(a)   **What is the amount paid through the bank account to trade payables in the year?**

£_____

(b)   **Using the figures given above (including your answer to part (a), prepare the payables (purchase ledger) control account for the year ended 31 December 20X2, showing clearly discounts received as the balancing figure.**

Payables (Purchase ledger) control account

(c) The prepayment shown in the schedule is for rent.

Using the figures above, calculate the charge to the statement of profit or loss for the year.

Rent expense

(d) The accrual shown above is for electricity.

If the electricity charge to the statement of profit or loss for the year is £5,125, calculate the closing accrual.

Electricity expense

4 RELIABLE CARS

You are working on the accounts of Reliable Cars for the year ended 30 September 20X6. You have the following information:

Sales for the year ended 30 September 20X6

- Credit sales amounted to £46,000 net of sales tax
- Cash sales amounted to £212,000 net of sales tax
- All sales are standard rated for sales tax at 20%.

Payments from the bank account for the year ended 30 September 20X6

- Payroll expenses   £48,000
- Administration expenses   £6,400 ignore sales tax
- Vehicle running costs   £192,000 including sales tax at 20%
- Drawings   £41,800
- Sales tax   £17,300

Summary of balances available

Balance as at	30 September 20X5	30 September 20X6
Bank account	5,630	8,140
Trade receivables	4,120	5,710
Sales tax (credit balances)	4,200	4,575

(a) Calculate the figure for credit sales for entry into the receivables (sales ledger) control account?

£_____

(b) Using the figures given above (including your answer to part (a), prepare the sales ledger control account for the year ended 30 September 20X6, showing clearly the receipts paid into the bank as the balancing figure.

Receivables (Sales ledger) control account

(c) Calculate the cash sales inclusive of sales tax which have been paid into the bank account. All cash sales are banked.

£_____

(d) Show a summarised bank account for the year ended 30 September 20X6.

Bank account

5   I.T. SOLUTIONS

I.T. Solutions is owned by Justin Long and started trading on 1 October 20X8. You have been provided with the following summarised bank account, and are required to assist in the preparation of the first set of accounts for the year ended 30 September 20X9.

Bank summary for the year ended 30 September 20X9

Capital introduced	16,000	Rent of premises	8,000
Receipts from trade receivables	49,600	Payments to trade payables	18,160
		Travel expenses	4,300
		Administration expenses	3,270
		Drawings	28,000
		Balance c/d	3,870
	65,600		65,600

Additional information:

- Justin transferred his own vehicle into the business on 1 October 20X8. It was valued at £4,000.

- On 30 September 20X9, trade receivables owed £6,300.

- On 30 September 20X9, trade payables were owed £2,500. Total supplies during the year were £22,000.

(a)   Prepare the receivables (sales ledger) control account showing clearly the credit sales as the balancing figure.

Receivables (Sales ledger) control account

(b)   Prepare the payables (purchases ledger) control account showing clearly the discounts received as the balancing figure.

Payables (Purchases ledger) control account

(c) **Prepare the opening capital account as at 1 October 20X8, showing clearly all the capital introduced.**

Capital account

6 BYRNE

You are working on the financial statements of Byrne who runs a clothing business for the year ended 31 May 20X6. You have the following information:

Day book summaries:	Goods £	Sales tax £	Total £
Sales	270,000	54,000	324,000
Purchases	180,000	36,000	216,000

Balances as at:	31 May X5 £	31 May X6 £
Trade receivables	28,500	24,000
Trade payables	23,750	19,600

Further information:	Net £	Sales tax £	Total £
Office expenses	9,500	1,900	11,400
Office expenses are not included in the purchases day book			

Bank summary	Dr £		Cr £
Trade receivables	325,000	Balance b/d	1,756
Interest received	150	Travel expenses	13,600
Cash sales (inc sales tax)	36,000	Office expenses	11,400
		Trade payables	220,150
		HMRC for sales tax	26,715
		Drawings	45,000
		Payroll expenses	25,000
		Balance c/d	17,529
	361,150		361,150

(a)   Using the figures given above, prepare the receivables (sales ledger) control account for the year ended 31 May 20X6. Show clearly sales returns as the balancing figure.

Receivables (Sales ledger) control account

(b)   Using the figures given above, prepare the payables (purchase ledger) control account for the year ended 31 May 20X6.

Payables (Purchase ledger) control account

(c)   Find the closing balance for sales tax (VAT) by preparing the sales tax control account for the year ended 31 May 20X6. Use the figures given above.

Note: The business is not charged sales tax on its travel expenses.

		Balance b/d	8,300

INCOMPLETE RECORDS USING THE NET ASSET APPROACH, MARK-UP, MARGINS AND ETHICAL PRINCIPLES

7   PERCY

You are given the following information about a sole trader called Percy as at 31 March 20X2:

The value of assets and liabilities were:

- Non-current assets at carrying amount   £14,000
- Bank   £2,500
- Trade payables   £10,300
- Opening capital (at 1 April 20X1)   £3,700
- Drawings for the year   £1,500

There were no other assets or liabilities.

(a) Calculate the profit for the year ended 30 March 20X2.

£_____

(b) Tick the boxes to show whether increases to the account balances would be a debit or credit.

You must choose ONE answer for EACH balance.

	Debit	Credit
Sales		
Prepayment		
Loan		
Accrual		
Trade receivables		

8 GROVER

You are given the following information about a sole trader called Grover as at 1 April 20X8:

The value of assets and liabilities were:

- Non-current assets at carrying amount   £17,150
- Trade receivables   £4,600
- Allowance for doubtful debts   £350
- Prepayments   £200
- Bank overdraft   £600
- Trade payables   £3,750
- Accruals   £325
- Capital   £11,475

There were no other assets or liabilities, with the exception of part (a)

(a) Calculate the long term loan account balance as at 1 April 20X8.

£_____

(b) Calculate the accumulated depreciation as at 1 April 20X8 if the non-current asset cost is £75,000.

£_____

(c) On 1 June 20X8 a piece of equipment is disposed of and the proceeds received by cheque.

Tick the boxes to show what effect this transaction will have on the balances. You must choose ONE answer for EACH line.

	Debit	Credit	No change
Non-current assets cost			
Accumulated depreciation			
Trade receivables			
Trade payables			
Bank			

9   CHIRON

You are given the following information about a sole trader called Chiron as at 31 January 20X5:

The value of assets and liabilities were:

- Non-current assets at cost   £10,000
- Trade receivables   £2,000
- Loan   £7,500
- Closing capital (at 31 January 20X5)   £3,500

There were no other assets or liabilities.

(a)   Calculate the amount of accumulated depreciation at the year end 31 January 20X5

£_____

(b)   Chiron sells goods at a mark-up of 25%. What would be the gross profit on a sales price of £11,000?

£_____

10   PARKER

You are given the following information about the business of Parker, a sole trader, as at 1 April 20X8:

The value of assets and liabilities were:

- Non-current assets at cost   £25,725
- Non-current asset accumulated depreciation   £8,670
- Trade receivables after allowance for doubtful debts   £4,790
- Prepayments   £190
- Long-term loan   £7,410
- Trade payables   £4,250
- Accruals   £360
- Capital   £10,130

There were no other assets or liabilities, with the exception of part (a)

(a)   Calculate the bank balance as at 1 April 20X8.

£_____

(b)   Calculate the trade receivables figure as at 1 April 20X8 if the allowance for doubtful debts is £480.

£_____

(c)   On 1 June 20X8 a piece of equipment is disposed of and the proceeds received in cash.

Tick the boxes to show what effect this transaction will have on the balances. You must choose ONE answer for EACH line.

	Debit	Credit	No change
Non-current assets cost			
Accumulated depreciation			
Trade receivables			
Bank balance			
Cash balance			

11   ANNABETH

You are given the following information about a sole trader called Annabeth as at 30 September:

The following balances are available:

Assets and liabilities as at:	30 Sept 20X3 £
Plant and equipment at cost	19,000
Plant and equipment accumulated depreciation	5,600
Inventory at cost	2,890
Cash	560
Bank	2,310
Prepayment for rent	550
Payables for materials	1,720
Accrual for travel expenses	380

Calculate the figure for capital as at 30 September 2003.

£_____

12   RUBICON

You make an entry for two transactions in a sole trader's accounts.

The table below shows the total assets and liabilities before and after the transactions:

Balances:	Before £	After £
Total assets	42,135	43,385
Total liabilities	28,653	29,273

Calculate the amount by which the capital balance has changed as a result of the transactions.

£_____

13   LUKE

Luke sells office equipment. He buys a photocopier for £900.

(a)   **What would the selling price be, excluding sales tax, if a 40% mark-up was applied?**

(b)   **What would the selling price be, excluding sales tax, if the sales margin was 40%?**

14   MARK UPPS AND MARGE INNS

Mark Upps and Marge Inns sell kitchen equipment and fittings.

(a)   **If they buy a gas cooker for £825 excluding sales tax, what would the selling price be, excluding sales tax, if a 40% mark-up was applied?**

£_____

(b)   **If they buy a gas cooker for £825 excluding sales tax, what would the selling price be, excluding sales tax, if the sales margin was 40%?**

£_____

(c)   **If they buy a freezer for £250 excluding sales tax, what would the profit be, excluding sales tax, if a 20% mark-up was applied?**

£_____

(d)   **If they buy a freezer for £250 excluding sales tax, what would the profit be, excluding sales tax, if the sales margin was 20%?**

£_____

(e)   **If they sell a dishwasher for £455 excluding sales tax, what would the purchase price be, excluding sales tax, if a 30% mark-up was included in the selling price?**

£_____

(f)   **If they sell a dishwasher for £455 excluding sales tax, what would the purchase price be, excluding sales tax, if a 30% sales margin was included in the selling price?**

£_____

15   CALEB

During the year ended 31 March 20X9, Caleb, a sole trader, made sales of £680,000 and operates with a mark-up on cost of 30%. Inventory at 1 April 20X8 was £52,326 and Caleb made purchases of £519,800 during the year.

Using this information, complete the following:

(a)   Calculate the cost of goods sold for the year ended 31 March 20X9. Show your answer to the nearest whole £.

£_____

(b)   Calculate the value of the inventory at 31 March 20X9.

£_____

16   ROSEMARY

During the year ended 30 September 20X7, Rosemary, a sole trader, made sales of £1,280,000 and made a sales margin of 25% on these. Rosemary made purchases of £970,200 during the year ended 30 September 20X7 and inventory was valued at £98,006 at the period end.

Using this information, complete the following:

(a)   Calculate the cost of goods sold for the year ended 30 September 20X7.

£_____

(b)   Calculate the value of the inventory at 1 October 20X6.

£_____

17   RTL PARTNERSHIP

You are working on the final accounts of RTL Partnership.

Your manager has asked you to check the amount recorded for accrued rental income for RTL Partnership. He explained that he would have completed the task himself but he believes it would be good experience for you and he has other work that he needs to complete today. You do not have any experience of calculating accrued income in the workplace or at college. Your manager requires the work to be completed by the end of the day.

What should you do? Choose one of the following options:

- Call your friend, who is an accountant, and ask her to help you complete the task.

- Explain the situation to your manager and ask if there is another person in the organisation who can help you.

- Call RTL Partnership and tell them that the deadline is going to be missed.

- Complete the task to the best of your ability.

18 OBJECTIVITY

Which two of the following situations present a threat to objectivity?

1   Joe is an accountant who is the Chief Financial Officer of Trax Corp. He leaves the company after he is offered a partnership position in HDI Partnership, an audit firm. After nine months of working at the firm, he is made the engagement partner on the Trax Corp audit.

2   Olivia is an accountant in charge of preparing financial statements for Choccy Chocolate, a business owned by Ben, a sole trader. Olivia asks for Choccy Chocolate's records to support its payables and receivables, but Ben says it will be too much work to get. Ben tells Olivia that he will employ another accountant unless she simply uses the numbers in the accounting system.

3   Justin is a junior auditor at a small auditing firm. He is working on the accounts of John and James, a partnership. He is suspicious about a payment to a supplier shown in the partnership's cashbook so John offers to obtain proof of payment from the bank.

4   Rachel's manager has asked you to a meeting to go through your goals for next year. Rachel asks her manager to send her a meeting request by email so that she can check her calendar and see when she is free.

19 LISA

Lisa is an AAT member working for a small accountancy practice.

She has received a call from a property agent asking for the following information about a client:

- The client's accounts for the previous three years

- An assurance that the client will be able to meet the rent for a proposed property rental.

(a)   What action should Lisa take, with regards to giving the agent the accounts for the previous three years? Choose one option.

- Lisa should obtain authority from the client to give the financial information

- Lisa should provide the information to the property agent as soon as possible

- Lisa should do nothing and hope that the property agent will not chase her up

- Lisa should provide the information by email and copy the client into the email

(b)   What action should Lisa take, with regards to giving the agent an assurance the client will be able to pay.

- She should tell the agent that the client will definitely be able to pay the rent

- It is not possible to give an assurance regarding the client's ability to pay the rent

- She should tell the agent that the client will not be able to meet the rent payments

- She should arrange a meeting with the agent to go through the client's accounts

SOLE TRADER STATEMENT OF FINANCIAL POSITION

20   PG TRADING

You have the following trial balance for a sole trader known as PG Trading. All the necessary year-end adjustments have been made.

PG Trading has a policy of showing trade receivables net of any allowance for doubtful debts.

The statement of profit or loss for PG Trading shows a profit of £7,900 for the period.

(a)   Prepare a statement of financial position for the business for the year ended 30 September 20X7.

PG Trading		
Trial balance as at 30 September 20X7		
	Dr £	**Cr £**
Accruals		6,000
Bank	5,000	
Capital		20,000
Drawings	3,000	
Closing inventory	11,000	11,000
Depreciation charge	1,800	
Allowance for doubtful debt adjustment	800	
General expenses	6,400	
Machinery at cost	15,900	
Machinery accumulated depreciation		5,800
Opening inventory	9,800	
Prepayments	5,100	
Allowance for doubtful debts		800
Purchases	46,000	
Purchases ledger control account		15,900
Rent	12,000	
Sales		78,700
Sales ledger control account	17,900	
VAT		1,500
Wages	5,000	
	139,700	139,700

PG Trading			
Statement of financial position as at 30 September 20X7			
	£	£	£
Non-current assets	**Cost**	**Depreciation**	**Carrying amount**
Current assets			
Current liabilities			
Net current assets			
Net assets			
Financed by:			
Opening capital			
Add:			
Less:			
Closing capital			

(b) Using your answer to part (a), what will be the opening capital balance on 1 October 20X7?

£_____

21 INVENTORY TRADING

You have the following trial balance for a sole trader known as Inventory Trading. All the necessary year-end adjustments have been made.

Inventory Trading has a policy of showing trade receivables net of any allowance for doubtful debts.

The statement of profit or loss for Inventory Trading shows a profit of £15,000 for the period.

(a) **Prepare a statement of financial position for the business for the year ended 31 March 20X1.**

Inventory Trading		
Trial balance as at 31 March 20X1		
	Dr £	Cr £
Accruals		2,500
Administration expenses	40,000	
Bank	4,100	
Capital		74,390
Cash	670	
Closing inventory	20,000	20,000
Drawings	1,400	
Depreciation charge	3,600	
Disposal of non-current asset	3,500	
Motor vehicles at cost	39,000	
Motor vehicles accumulated depreciation		18,500
Opening inventory	25,400	
Allowance for doubtful debts		1,200
Allowance for doubtful debt adjustment	110	
Purchases	83,300	
Purchases ledger control account		28,500
Revenue		156,800
Sales ledger control account	78,920	
Selling expenses	5,890	
VAT		4,000
Total	305,890	305,890

Inventory Trading			
Statement of financial position as at 31 March 20X1			
	£	£	£
Non-current assets	**Cost**	**Depreciation**	**Carrying amount**
Current assets			
Current liabilities			
Net current assets			
Net assets			
Financed by:			
Opening capital			
Add:			
Less:			
Closing capital			

(b) **If there had been a prepayment balance in the trial balance, where would this be shown in the statement of financial position? Choose one option.**

- As a non-current asset.

- As a current liability.

- In the 'financed by' section.

- As a current asset.

22 WINSTON TRADING

You have the following trial balance for a sole trader known as Winston Trading. All the necessary year-end adjustments have been made.

Winston Trading has a policy of showing trade receivables net of any allowance for doubtful debts and showing trade payables and sundry payables as one total figure.

The statement of profit or loss for Winston Trading shows a profit of £8,810 for the period.

Prepare a statement of financial position for the business for the year ended 30 June 20X8.

Winston Trading Trial balance as at 30 June 20X8		
	Dr £	Cr £
Accruals		750
Bank		1,250
Capital		17,000
Closing inventory	7,850	7,850
Discounts received		900
Sundry payables		1,450
Purchase ledger control account		6,800
Depreciation charge	1,600	
Discounts allowed	345	
Allowance for doubtful debts adjustment	295	
Equipment accumulated depreciation		4,500
Wages	24,000	
Sales ledger control account	7,800	
Rent	5,250	
Revenue		164,000
Disposal		450
Prepayments	3,200	
Purchases	125,000	
Sales returns	1,500	
Opening inventory	3,450	
Equipment at cost	17,500	
Drawings	8,000	
General expenses	2,950	
Allowance for doubtful debts		840
VAT		2,950
	208,740	208,740

Winston Trading

Statement of financial position as at 30 June 20X8

	£	£	£
Non-current assets	**Cost**	**Depreciation**	**Carrying amount**
Current assets			
Current liabilities			
Net current assets			
Net assets			
Financed by:			
Opening capital			
Add:			
Less:			
Closing capital			

23   BALFOUR

You are preparing the statement of financial position for Balfour, a sole trader. All the necessary year-end adjustments have been made.

Balfour has a policy of showing trade receivables net of any allowance for doubtful debts. The statement of profit or loss for Balfour shows a loss of £4,350 for the period.

Prepare a statement of financial position for the business for the year ended 30 June 20X6.

Balfour		
Trial balance as at 30 June 20X6		
	Dr **£**	**Cr** **£**
Accruals		3,150
Administration expenses	45,000	
Bank		2,250
Capital		85,000
Cash	500	
Closing inventory	17,500	17,500
Depreciation charge	9,000	
Disposal of non-current asset		1,500
Motor vehicles at cost	45,000	
Motor vehicles accumulated depreciation		20,000
Opening inventory	15,000	
Allowance for doubtful debts		1,450
Allowance for doubtful debts adjustment	200	
Purchases	75,000	
Purchases ledger control account		23,750
Revenue		130,000
Sales ledger control account	68,550	
Selling expenses	9,150	
Drawings	3,200	
VAT		3,500
Total	288,100	288,100

Balfour			
Statement of financial position as at 30 June 20X6			
	£	£	£
Non-current assets	**Cost**	**Depreciation**	**Carrying amount**
Current assets			
Current liabilities			
Net current assets			
Net assets			
Financed by:			
Opening capital			
Less:			
Less:			
Closing capital			

REPORTING REGULATIONS FOR DIFFERENT TYPES OF ORGANISATIONS, THE LEGAL AND REGULATORY FRAMEWORK

24   USERS OF THE FINAL ACCOUNTS

Link the users of final accounts on the left below with the most likely reason for their interest on the right.

| | | To make decisions regarding their investment |

| HMRC | | To assess the security of any loan |

| Shareholders | | To compare information from other organisations operating in the same sector |

| | | To assess the amount of tax payable by the business |

25   THE FQS

From the list below select the two fundamental qualitative characteristics of useful financial information

- Faithful representation
- Objectivity
- Communication
- Relevance
- Comparability
- Understandability

26   BORIS

You have worked on the accounts of Boris, a sole trader, for many years. In the last 5 years, Boris has made some quite substantial losses.

Based on this information, which of the following accounting concepts requires particular consideration when preparing the final accounts of Boris?

- Accruals
- Going concern
- Consistency
- None of the above

27   CHARITIES

State whether the following statements about charities are true or false.

(a)   To be classed as a charity, an organisation must meet the definition of a charity as set out in the Charities Act 2011.

(b)   Organisations which wish to be classed as charities need to be established for charitable purposes, meaning that it must be for the general benefit of HMRC.

28   INTERNATIONAL ACCOUNTING STANDARDS

Match each of the following International Accounting Standards with the relevant accounting rule.

IAS 1   IAS 2   IAS 16

Rules:

*   Inventories should be valued at the lower of cost and net realisable value.

*   Property, plant and equipment is measured at its cost and depreciated so that its depreciable amount is allocated over its useful economic life.

*   A complete set of financial statements must include a statement of profit or loss and a statement of financial position.

PARTNERSHIP ACCOUNTING

29   CELEBRATION CUPCAKES

You have the following information about a partnership:

*   The partners are Erica and Hayley, and the partnership sells cupcakes.

*   Anna was admitted to the partnership on 1 April 20X8 when she introduced £65,000 to the bank account.

*   Profit share, effective until 31 March 20X8

    –   Erica   60%

    –   Hayley   40%

*   Profit share, effective from 1 April 20X8

    –   Erica   40%

    –   Hayley   30%

    –   Anna   30%

*   Goodwill was valued at £40,000 on 31 March 20X8.

*   Goodwill is to be introduced into the partners' capital accounts on 31 March and then eliminated on 1 April.

Prepare the capital account for Erica, showing clearly the balance carried down as at 1 April 20X8.

Capital account – Erica

		Balance b/d	10,000

30 WYN, FRANCIS AND BILL

Wyn and Francis are in partnership, and have given you the following information.

- Bill was admitted to the partnership on 1 July 20X9 when he introduced £75,000 to the bank account.

- Profit share, effective until 30 June 20X9

  - Wyn 60%
  - Francis 40%

- Profit share, effective from 1 July 20X9

  - Wyn 40%
  - Francis 30%
  - Bill 30%

- Goodwill was valued at £45,000 on 30 June 20X9.

- Goodwill is to be introduced into the partners' capital accounts on 30 June and then eliminated on 1 July.

(a) **Prepare the goodwill account, clearly showing the introduction and elimination of goodwill.**

Goodwill

(b) **Prepare the capital account for Bill, clearly showing the carried forward balance.**

Capital account – Bill

31 FLORA, JASMINE AND MAVIS

You have the following information about a partnership:

- The partners are Flora and Jasmine, and the partnership arranges children's parties.

- Mavis joined the partnership on 1 May 20X7 when she introduced £128,000 into the business bank account.

- Profit share, effective until 30 April 20X7

  - Flora   35%

  - Jasmine   65%

- Profit share, effective from 1 May 20X7

  - Flora   25%

  - Jasmine   45%

  - Mavis   30%

- Goodwill was valued at £105,000 on 30 April 20X7.

- Goodwill is to be introduced into the partners' capital accounts on 30 April and then eliminated on 1 May.

(a) **Show the entries required to introduce the goodwill into the partnership accounting records.**

Account name	Dr	Cr

- Flora is thinking of leaving the partnership next year. It is estimated that Mavis' good reputation will have added £22,000 to the goodwill value by then.

(b) **Calculate the goodwill to be introduced into Flora's capital account at the time of her departure.**

£_____

32   PHIL, GEOFF AND JACK

Phil, Geoff and Jack are in partnership selling dog food.

- Jack retired from the partnership on 30 June 20X5. He has agreed that the partnership will pay what he is due from the bank account in full.

- Profit share, effective until 30 June 20X5

    - Phil   30%

    - Geoff   40%

    - Jack   30%

- Profit share, effective from 1 July 20X5

    - Phil   50%

    - Geoff   50%

- Goodwill was valued at £50,000 on 30 June 20X5

- Goodwill is to be introduced into the partners' capital accounts on 30 June and then eliminated on 1 July.

- At the 30 June 20X5 the partners had the following balances on their capital and current accounts:

    - Phil   £7,000 (capital a/c) and £11,000 (current a/c)

    - Geoff   £8,000 (capital a/c) and £9,000 (current a/c)

    - Jack   £9,000 (capital a/c) and £7,000 (current a/c)

(a)   Prepare the capital account for Jack, showing clearly the transfer from the current account and the amount paid to Jack on his retirement.

Capital account – Jack

		Balance b/d	9,000

(b)   Complete the following sentence by selecting the appropriate account.

If the partnership was unable to pay Jack the balance on his capital account on his retirement, the balance could be transferred to a

1   Non-current asset account

2   Loan account

3   Trade payable account

33   DAN, KIM AND TED

Dan, Kim and Ted are in partnership within the building trade, preparing accounts to the year ended 31 March.

On 30 November 20X4, Dan retired from the partnership. You have the following information about the partnership agreement.

- Profit share, effective until 30 November 20X4

  – Dan   40%

  – Kim   30%

  – Ted   30%

- Profit share, effective from 1 December 20X4

  – Kim   50%

  – Ted   50%

- Goodwill was valued at £100,000 on 30 November 20X4

- Goodwill is to be eliminated from the accounts

Prepare the goodwill account for the partnership for the year ended 31 March 20X5, showing clearly the individual transfers to each of the partners' capital accounts.

Goodwill

34   RACHAEL, ED AND MATTY

You have the following information about a partnership business:

The financial year ends on 30 June.

- The partners are Rachael, Ed and Matty.

- Partners' annual salaries

  – Rachael   £18,000

  – Ed   nil

  – Matty   £36,000

- Partners' interest on capital

  – Rachael   £2,000 per annum

  – Ed   £2,000 per annum

  – Matty   £2,000 per annum

- Partners' sales commission earned during the year
  - Rachael £8,250
  - Ed £6,800
  - Matty £4,715
- Profit share
  - Rachael 40%
  - Ed 40%
  - Matty 20%

The statement of profit or loss for the partnership shows a profit for the year ended 30 June 20X9 of £220,000 before appropriations.

Prepare the appropriation account for the partnership for the year ended 30 June 20X9. Enter zeros where appropriate and use minus signs for deductions.

Partnership Appropriation account for the year ended 30 June 20X9

	£
Profit for the year	
Salaries:	
Rachael	
Ed	
Matty	
Interest on capital:	
Rachael	
Ed	
Matty	
Sales commission:	
Rachael	
Ed	
Matty	
Profit available for distribution	

Profit share:	
Rachael	
Ed	
Matty	
Total residual profit distributed	

35   NYAH, SHAUNA AND MOLLIE

You have the following information about a partnership business:

- The financial year ends on 31 March.

- The partners are Nyah, Shauna and Mollie.

- Partners' annual salaries
    - Nyah   £25,000
    - Shauna   £19,000
    - Mollie   nil

- Partners' sales commission earned during the year
    - Nyah   £1,100 per annum
    - Shauna   £1,100 per annum
    - Mollie   £1,100 per annum

- Profit share
    - Nyah   35%
    - Shauna   20%
    - Mollie   45%

The statement of profit or loss for the partnership shows a profit for the year ended 31 March 20Y0 of £70,000 before appropriations.

Prepare the appropriation account for the partnership for the year ended 31 March 20Y0. Enter zeros where appropriate and use minus signs for deductions.

Partnership Appropriation account for the year ended 31 March 20Y0

	£
Profit for the year	
Salaries:	
Nyah	
Shauna	
Mollie	
Sales commission	
Nyah	
Shauna	
Mollie	
Profit available for distribution	

	£
Profit share:	
Nyah	
Shauna	
Mollie	
Total residual profit distributed	

36 EDWARD, JAKE AND BELLA

This task is about partnership accounts. You have the following information about a partnership business:

- The financial year ends on 31 December.

- The partners are Edward, Jake and Bella.

- Partners' annual salaries

    - Edward   £30,000

    - Jake   nil

    - Bella   £21,000

- Partners' sales commission earned during the year

    - Edward   £3,000 per annum

    - Jake   £3,000 per annum

    - Bella   £3,200 per annum

- Partners' interest on drawings

    - Edward   £1,880 per annum

    - Jake   £2,870 per annum

    - Bella   nil

- Profit share

    - Edward   50%

    - Jake   20%

    - Bella   30%

Profit for the year for the year ended 31 December 20X0 was £52,000 before appropriations.

Prepare the appropriation account for the partnership for the year ended 31 December 20X0. Enter zeros where appropriate and use minus signs for deductions.

Partnership Appropriation account for the year ended 31 December 20X0

	£
Profit for the year	
Salaries:	
Edward	
Jake	
Bella	
Sales commission:	
Edward	
Jake	
Bella	
Interest on drawings:	
Edward	
Jake	
Bella	
Residual profit / loss	

Profit / loss share:	
Edward	
Jake	
Bella	
Total residual profit / loss distributed	

37 GARY, MARK AND ROBBIE

Gary, Mark and Robbie are in partnership, preparing accounts to the year ended 30 June. You are given the following information:

- The financial year ends on 30 June.

- Partners' annual salaries

    - Gary   £18,000

    - Mark   nil

    - Robbie   £36,000

- Partners' capital account balances as at 30 June 20X9

    - Gary   £100,000

    - Mark   £60,000

    - Robbie   £75,000

- Interest on capital is charged at 5% per annum on the capital account balance at the end of the financial year.

- The partners share the remaining profit of £80,000 as follows:

  - Gary 40%

  - Mark 40%

  - Robbie 20%

- Partners' drawings for the year

  - Gary £34,000

  - Mark £30,000

  - Robbie £58,000

Prepare the current accounts for the partners for the year ended 30 June 20X9, showing clearly the balances carried down.

Current accounts

	Gary £	Mark £	Robbie £		Gary £	Mark £	Robbie £
				Balance b/d	2,000	1,500	250

38 JOHN, JACKIE AND TEGAN

John, Jackie and Tegan are in partnership, producing accounts to the year ended 30 June. You are given the following information:

- Partners' annual salaries

  - John £11,000

  - Jackie £16,500

  - Tegan nil

- Partners' capital account balances as at 30 June 20X8

  - John £47,500

  - Jackie £56,000

  - Tegan £56,000

- Interest on capital is charged at 4% per annum on the capital account balance at the end of the financial year.

- The partners share the **remaining** profit of £75,000 as follows:

  - John 35%

  - Jackie 45%

  - Tegan 20%

- Partners' drawings for the year
  - John   £18,000
  - Jackie   £35,000
  - Tegan   £12,750

Prepare the current accounts for the partners for the year ended 30 June 20X8. Show clearly the balances carried down.

Current accounts

	John £	Jackie £	Tegan £		John £	Jackie £	Tegan £
Balance b/d	750			Balance b/d		1,900	600

39 LOUIS, CHERYL AND SIMON

Louis, Cheryl and Simon are in partnership producing accounts to the year ended 31 December. You are given the following information:

- Partners' annual salaries
  - Louis   £30,000
  - Cheryl   nil
  - Simon   £21,000

- Partners' capital account balances as at 31 December 20X9
  - Louis   £50,000
  - Cheryl   £50,000
  - Simon   £20,000

- Interest on capital is charged at 2% per annum on the capital account balance at the end of the financial year.

- The partners share the remaining profit of £60,000 as follows:
  - Louis   50%
  - Cheryl   20%
  - Simon   30%

- Partners' drawings for the year
  - Louis   £25,000
  - Cheryl   £10,200
  - Simon   £31,000

Prepare the current accounts for the partners for the year ended 31 December 20X9. Show clearly the balances carried down.

Current accounts

	Louis £	Cheryl £	Simon £		Louis £	Cheryl £	Simon £
				Balance b/d	3,500	1,800	1,000

40   DEREK, JIN AND AHMED

Derek, Jin and Ahmed are in business together sharing profits in the ratio 3:3:4 after providing for salaries for Derek and Jin of £20,000 and £24,000 respectively. The partners each receive interest on their capital balances and pay interest of on their drawings as outlined below. The profit for the year to 31 March 20X8 is £254,000 before providing for salaries or interest.

	Interest on capital £	Interest on drawings £
Derek	8,000	4,600
Jin	7,200	3,800
Ahmed	10,560	4,800

Prepare the appropriation account for the partnership for the year ended 31 March 20X8. Enter zeros where appropriate and use minus signs for deductions.

Partnership Appropriation account for the year ended 31 March 20X8

	£
Profit for the year	
Salaries:	
Derek	
Jin	
Ahmed	
Interest on capital:	
Derek	
Jin	
Ahmed	
Interest on drawings:	
Derek	
Jin	
Ahmed	
Profit available for distribution	

Profit share:	
Derek	
Jin	
Ahmed	
Total residual profit distributed	

41   JACOB AND OLIVER

Jacob and Oliver are in partnership sharing profits equally and compiling financial statements to 31 December each year. They are both paid a salary of £20,000 each year. They receive both interest on their capital balances, sales commission on their sales made during the year and pay interest on their drawings which are all outlined below:

	Interest on capital	Interest on drawings	Sales commission earned
	£	£	£
Jacob	2,800	2,275	1,560
Oliver	6,250	0	2,690

The profit for the year ended 31 December 20X8 is £182,225 before appropriations.

Prepare the appropriation account for the partnership for the year ended 31 December 20X8. Enter zeros where appropriate and use minus signs for deductions.

Partnership Appropriation account for the year ended 31 December 20X8:

	£
Profit for the year	
Salaries:	
Jacob	
Oliver	
Interest on capital:	
Jacob	
Oliver	
Sales commission:	
Jacob	
Oliver	
Interest on drawings:	
Jacob	
Oliver	
Profit available for distribution	

Profit share:	
Jacob	
Oliver	
Total residual profit distributed	

PARTNERSHIP STATEMENT OF PROFIT OR LOSS

42   R & R TRADING

You have the following trial balance for a partnership known as R & R Trading. All the necessary year-end adjustments have been made.

The partners are Rita and Richard; they share profits 55:45 with Rita taking the larger share.

R & R Trading have a policy of including sales returns in the sales figure and purchases returns in the purchases figure.

Use a minus sign to indicate the following ONLY:

- a net loss for the year

- the closing inventory figure.

(a) Prepare a statement of profit or loss for the business for the year ended 30 September 20X7.

R & R Trading		
Trial balance as at 30 September 20X7		
	Dr £	**Cr** £
Accruals		4,100
Bank	3,500	
Closing inventory	19,500	19,500
Capital – Rita		5,050
Capital – Richard		5,050
Current– Rita		920
Current – Richard	745	
Depreciation charge	7,100	
Discounts allowed	1,350	
Drawings – Rita	6,000	
Drawings – Richard	5,000	
General expenses	26,100	
Machinery at cost	26,175	
Machinery accumulated depreciation		15,000
Opening inventory	17,700	
Sales returns	2,200	
Prepayments	4,600	
Purchases	98,000	
Purchases ledger control account		32,000
Rent	7,300	
Revenue		173,050
Sales ledger control account	26,400	
VAT		5,500
Wages	8,500	
	260,170	260,170

R & R Trading

Statement of profit or loss for the year ended 30 September 20X7

	£	£
Revenue		
Cost of goods sold		
Gross profit		
Less:		
Total expenses		
Profit for the year		

(b) **Calculate Rita's share of the profit or loss and her final current account balance.**

	£
Rita's share of the profit or loss	
Rita's final current account balance	

43 OSMOND PARTNERSHIP

You have the following trial balance for a partnership known as Osmond Partnership. All the necessary year-end adjustments have been made.

The partners are Aimee and Heather who share profits and losses equally.

Osmond Partnership have a policy of including sales returns in the sales figure and purchases returns in the purchases figure.

Use a minus sign to indicate the following ONLY:

- a net loss for the year

- the closing inventory figure.

(a) **Prepare a statement of profit or loss for the partnership for the year ended 31 March 20X1.**

Osmond Partnership		
Trial balance as at 31 March 20X1		
	Dr **£**	**Cr** **£**
Accruals		750
Bank		1,250
Capital – Aimee		8,000
Capital – Heather		7,500
Closing inventory	7,850	7,850
Discounts received		900
Current – Aimee		1,000
Current – Heather	400	
Sundry payables		1,450
Purchase ledger control account		6,800
Depreciation charge	1,600	
Discounts allowed	345	
Irrecoverable debt expense	295	
Drawings – Aimee	3,250	
Drawings – Heather	3,250	
Allowance for doubtful debts		840
Equipment at cost	18,100	
Equipment accumulated depreciation		4,500
Prepayments	3,200	
Sales ledger control account	7,800	
Wages	24,000	
Rent	5,250	
Disposal		450
Sales returns	1,500	
Opening inventory	3,450	
Purchases	125,000	
General expenses	2,950	
Revenue		164,000
VAT		2,950
	———	———
	208,240	208,240
	———	———

Osmond Partnership		
Statement of profit or loss for the year ended 31 March 20X1		
	£	£
Revenue		
Cost of goods sold		
Gross profit		
Add:		
Total sundry income		
Less:		
Total expenses		
Profit for the year		

(b) **Using your answer to part (a), calculate Heather's share of the profit or loss and her final current account balance.**

	£
Heather's share of the profit or loss	
Heather's final current account balance	

44 PERSEPHONE'S

You are preparing the statement of profit or loss for Persephone's for the year ended 30 June 20X8.

The partners are Tina and Cher. They share profits and losses 60:40, with Tina taking the larger share.

All the necessary year-end adjustments have been made.

Use a minus sign to indicate the following ONLY:

- a net loss for the year

- the closing inventory figure.

(a) **Using the trial balance provided, prepare a statement of profit or loss for the partnership for the year ended 30 June 20X8.**

Persephone's

Trial balance as at 30 June 20X8

	Dr £	Cr £
Accruals		2,500
Bank	3,500	
Capital – Tina		2,050
Capital – Cher		2,050
Closing inventory	9,800	9,800
Depreciation charge	800	
Allowance for doubtful debts adjustment		1,000
Current – Tina		2,257
Current – Cher		3,750
Drawings – Tina	2,054	
Drawings – Cher	2,553	
General expenses	8,200	
Machinery at cost	10,500	
Machinery accumulated depreciation		4,300
Opening inventory	9,100	
Prepayments	6,100	
Purchases	38,700	
Purchases ledger control account		12,500
Rent	5,900	
Revenue		85,000
Allowance for doubtful debts		1,850
Sales ledger control account	23,350	
VAT		2,000
Wages	8,500	
	129,057	129,057

Persephone's		
Statement of profit or loss for the year ended 30 June 20X8		
	£	£
Revenue		
Cost of goods sold		
Gross profit		
Plus:		
Less:		
Total expenses		
Profit for the year		

(b) Calculate Tina's and Cher's closing current account balances in the table below as well as showing their capital balances.

	Tina (£)	Cher (£)	Total (£)
Current account			
Capital account			

45 SUAREZ PARTNERSHIP

You are preparing the statement of profit or loss for the Suarez Partnership for the year ended 30 June 20X6. The partners are Louis and Emilio. They share profits equally.

All the necessary year-end adjustments have been made. Suarez Partnership have a policy of including sales returns in the sales figure and purchases returns in the purchases figure.

Use a minus sign to indicate the following ONLY:

- a net loss for the year
- the closing inventory figure.

(a) **Prepare a statement of profit or loss for the partnership for the year ended 30 June 20X6.**

Suarez Partnership		
Trial balance as at 30 June 20X6		
	Dr **£**	**Cr** **£**
Accruals		1,375
Bank		900
Capital – Louis		4,160
Capital – Emilio		3,000
Closing inventory	12,500	12,500
Depreciation charge	925	
Disposal of non-current asset		225
Drawings – Louis	2,500	
Drawings – Emilio	2,500	
Current – Louis		1,500
Current – Emilio	200	
General expenses	9,300	
Machinery at cost	8,000	
Machinery accumulated depreciation		5,200
Opening inventory	13,100	
Prepayments	1,250	
Purchases	70,600	
Purchases returns		2,350
Purchases ledger control account		11,375
Rent	6,000	
Revenue		108,000
Sales ledger control account	17,800	
Sales tax		6,090
Wages	12,000	
	156,675	156,675

Suarez Partnership

Statement of profit or loss for the year ended 30 June 20X6

	£	£
Revenue		
Cost of goods sold		
Gross profit		
Plus:		
Less:		
Total expenses		
Profit for the year		

(b) Calculate Louis' and Emilio's closing current account balances in the table below as well as showing their capital balances.

	Louis (£)	Emilio (£)	Total (£)
Current account			
Capital account			

(c) Identify whether the following statements about the preparation of the final accounts for a limited company are true or false.

- The taxation charge for a limited company is shown as an expense in the statement of profit or loss.

- A limited company must prepare the final accounts every six months.

- Only the carrying amount of each type of non-current asset is shown on the face of the statement of financial position.

UNDERPINNING KNOWLEDGE

46 SHORT FORM QUESTIONS

1 **A trial balance guarantees there are no errors in the accounting records.**

(a) True

(b) False

2 **Which of the following is best described as a non-current asset. Choose ONE answer.**

(a) A car purchased for resale by a car dealer

(b) A positive bank account (debit)

(c) A car for use by the company salesman

(d) An insurance invoice covering the following 12 month period

3 **Which of the following is best described as a current liability? Choose ONE answer.**

(a) An item of inventory that will be sold in the next couple of months

(b) A delivery van that will be sold next week

(c) A loan that will be paid back to the bank in the next few months

(d) A sales invoice for goods sold to a customer that will be paid in the next month

4 **When extending the trial balance, if the debit column of the statement of profit or loss is £125,000 and the credit column is £137,000, what entry would be required?**

(a) None

(b) Dr statement of profit or loss £12,000/Cr statement of financial position £12,000

(c) Dr statement of profit or loss £12,000

(d) Dr statement of financial position £12,000/Cr statement of profit or loss £12,000

5 **Referring back to question 4, is this a profit or a loss?**

(a) Profit

(b) Loss

6 **For each of the transactions below, tick whether the account balance would be debited, credited or would not change. Choose ONE answer for each line.**

(a) A sole trader makes a credit sale (ignore sales tax)

	Debit	Credit	No change
Revenue			
Loan			
Non-current assets			
Trade receivables			

(b)   A sole trader decides to write off an irrecoverable debt

	Debit	**Credit**	**No change**
Trade payables			
Inventory			
Irrecoverable debt expense			
Trade receivables			

(c)   A sole trader purchases a new computer on credit for use in the business

	Debit	**Credit**	**No change**
Discount allowed			
Sundry payables			
Non-current assets			
Inventory			

(d)   A sole trader accounts for the cash received on disposal of a motor vehicle

	Debit	**Credit**	**No change**
Motor vehicles repairs			
Motor vehicles depreciation expense			
Disposal of motor vehicles account			
Bank			

(e)   A sole trader pays transport costs to have goods delivered to his premises

	Debit	**Credit**	**No change**
Bank			
Carriage inwards			
Carriage outwards			
Purchases			

(f)   A sole trader pays transport costs to have goods delivered to customers

	Debit	**Credit**	**No change**
Bank			
Carriage inwards			
Carriage outwards			
Sales			

Section 2

ANSWERS TO PRACTICE QUESTIONS

INCOMPLETE RECORDS AND RECONSTRUCTION OF LEDGER ACCOUNTS

1   A CATERING BUSINESS

(a)   **Receivables (Sales ledger) control account**

Balance b/d	26,000		
SDB	289,200	Bank	294,875
		Discount allowed	8,325
		Balance c/d	12,000
	315,200		315,200

(b)   **Sales tax control**

PDB	18,800	Balance b/d	4,300
Office expenses	1,600	SDB	48,200
Bank	27,525	Cash sales	3,000
Balance c/d	7,575		
	55,500		55,500

2   LOCKE TRADING

(a)   **Payables (Purchases ledger) control account**

Bank	105,200	Balance b/d	8,700
Discounts received	3,190	PDB	112,320
Contra with SCLA	500		
Balance c/d	12,130		
	121,020		121,020

(b)   **Sales tax control**

PDB	18,720	Balance b/d	2,300
Admin expenses	7,400	SDB	39,000
Bank	6,450		
Balance c/d	8,730		
	41,300		41,300

3   FIRST POSITION BALLET SUPPLIES

(a)   £98,500

(b)   **Payables (Purchases ledger) control account**

Bank	98,500	Balance b/d	12,400
PRDB	9,600	PDB	110,400
Discount received	4,900		
Balance c/d	9,800		
	122,800		122,800

(c)   **Rent expense**

Balance b/d	300	Profit or loss	9,850
Bank	10,000	Balance c/d	450
	10,300		10,300

(d)   **Electricity expense**

Bank	5,000	Balance b/d	250
Balance c/d	375	Profit or loss	5,125
	5,375		5,375

4   **RELIABLE CARS**

(a)   £55,200

(b)   **Receivables (Sales ledger) control account**

Balance b/d	4,120	Bank	53,610
Credit sales	55,200	Balance c/d	5,710
	59,320		59,320

(c)   £254,400

(d)   **Bank account**

Balance b/d	5,630	Payroll expenses	48,000
SLCA	53,610	Administration expenses	6,400
Cash sales	254,400	Vehicle running costs	192,000
		Drawings	41,800
		Sales tax	17,300
		Balance c/d	8,140
	313,640		313,640

5   **I.T. SOLUTIONS**

(a)   **Receivables (Sales ledger) control account**

		Bank	49,600
		Balance c/d	6,300
Credit sales	55,900		
	55,900		55,900

(b)   **Payables (Purchases ledger) control account**

Bank	18,160	Purchases	22,000
Balance c/d	2,500		
Discounts received	1,340		
	22,000		22,000

(c)   **Capital account**

		Bank	16,000
		Motor vehicle cost	4,000
Balance c/d	20,000		
	20,000		20,000

6   BYRNE

(a)   **Receivables (Sales ledger) control account**

Balance b/d	28,500	Bank	325,000
SDB	324,000	Sales returns	3,500
		Balance c/d	24,000
	352,500		352,500

(b)   **Payables (Purchase ledger) control account**

Bank	220,150	Balance b/d	23,750
Balance c/d	19,600	PDB	216,000
	239,750		239,750

(c)   **Sales tax control**

PDB	36,000	Balance b/d	8,300
Office expenses	1,900	SDB	54,000
Bank	26,715	Cash sales	6,000
Balance c/d	3,685		
	68,300		68,300

INCOMPLETE RECORDS USING THE NET ASSET APPROACH, MARK-UP, MARGINS AND ETHICAL PRINCIPLES

7 **PERCY**

(a)   £4,000

(b)

	Debit	**Credit**
Sales		✓
Prepayment	✓	
Loan		✓
Accrual		✓
Trade receivables	✓	

8 **GROVER**

(a)   £5,450

(b)   £57,850

(c)

	Debit	**Credit**	**No change**
Non-current assets cost		✓	
Accumulated depreciation	✓		
Trade receivables			✓
Trade payables			✓
Bank	✓		

9 **CHIRON**

(a)   £1,000

(b)   £2,200

10 PARKER

(a) £115

(b) £5,270

(c)

	Debit	Credit	No change
Non-current assets cost		✓	
Accumulated depreciation	✓		
Trade receivables			✓
Bank balance			✓
Cash balance	✓		

11 ANNABETH

£17,610

12 RUBICON

£630

Assets – Liabilities = Capital

Before £42,135 – £28,653 = £13,482

After   £43,385 – £29,273 = £14,112

Increased by £630

13 LUKE

(a) 900 + 40% = £1,260

(b) 900 × 100/60 = £1,500

14 MARK UPPS AND MARGE INNS

(a) £825 × 140/100 = £1,155

(b) £825 × 100/60 = £1,375

(c) £250 × 20/100 = £50

(d) £250 × 20/80 = £62.50

(e) £455 × 100/130 = £350

(f) £455 × 70/100 = £318.50

15 CALEB

(a) £680,000 × 100/130 = £523,077

(b) £52,326 + £519,800 – £523,077 = £49,049

16 ROSEMARY

(a)   £1,280,000 × 75/100 = £960,000

(b)   £960,000 − (£970,200 − £98,006) = £87,806

17 RTL PARTNERSHIP

- Explain the situation to your manager and ask if there is another person in the organisation who can help you.

18 OBJECTIVITY

1   Joe is an accountant who is the Chief Financial Officer of Trax Corp. He leaves the company after he is offered a partnership position in HDI Partnership, an audit firm. After nine months of working at the firm, he is made the engagement partner on the Trax Corp audit. **This would give rise to familiarity and intimidation threats.**

2   Olivia is an accountant in charge of preparing financial statements for Choccy Chocolate, a business owned by Ben, a sole trader. Olivia asks for Choccy Chocolate's records to support its payables and receivables, but Ben says it will be too much work to get. Ben tells Olivia that he will employ another accountant unless she simply uses the numbers in the accounting system. **This would give rise to an intimidation threat.**

19 LISA

(a)   Lisa should obtain authority from the client to give the financial information

(b)   It is not possible to give an assurance regarding the client's ability to pay the rent

SOLE TRADER STATEMENT OF FINANCIAL POSITION

20 PG TRADING

(a)

PG Trading			
Statement of financial position as at 30 September 20X7			
	£	£	£
Non-current assets	Cost	Depreciation	Carrying amount
Machinery	15,900	5,800	10,100
Current assets			
Inventory		11,000	
Trade receivables (£17,900 – £800)		17,100	
Bank		5,000	
Prepayments		5,100	
		38,200	
Current liabilities			
Trade payables	15,900		
Accruals	6,000		
VAT	1,500		
		23,400	
Net current assets			14,800
Net assets			24,900
Financed by:			
Opening capital			20,000
Add: Net profit			7,900
Less: Drawings			3,000
Closing capital			24,900

(b)   £24,900

21   INVENTORY TRADING

(a)

Inventory Trading			
Statement of financial position as at 31 March 20X1			
	£	£	£
Non-current assets	**Cost**	**Depreciation**	**Carrying amount**
Motor vehicles	39,000	18,500	20,500
Current assets			
Inventory		20,000	
Trade receivables (£78,920 – £1,200)		77,720	
Bank		4,100	
Cash		670	
		102,490	
Current liabilities			
Trade payables	28,500		
VAT	4,000		
Accruals	2,500		
		35,000	
Net current assets			67,490
Net assets			87,990
Financed by:			
Opening capital			74,390
Add: Net profit			15,000
Less: Drawings			1,400
Closing capital			87,990

(b)   As a current asset.

22   WINSTON TRADING

Winston Trading			
Statement of financial position as at 30 June 20X8			
	£	£	£
Non-current assets	**Cost**	**Depreciation**	**Carrying amount**
Equipment	17,500	4,500	13,000
Current assets			
Inventory		7,850	
Trade receivables (£7,800 – £840)		6,960	
Prepayments		3,200	
		18,010	
Current liabilities			
Payables (£6,800 + £1,450)	8,250		
VAT	2,950		
Accruals	750		
Bank	1,250		
		13,200	
Net current assets			4,810
Net assets			17,810
Financed by:			
Opening capital			17,000
Add: Net profit			8,810
Less: Drawings			8,000
Closing capital			17,810

23 BALFOUR

Balfour

Statement of financial position as at 30 June 20X6

	£	£	£
Non-current assets	**Cost**	**Depreciation**	**Carrying amount**
Motor vehicles	45,000	20,000	25,000
Current assets			
Inventory		17,500	
Trade receivables (£68,550 – £1,450)		67,100	
Cash		500	
		85,100	
Current liabilities			
Bank	2,250		
Trade payables	23,750		
Accruals	3,150		
VAT	3,500		
		32,650	
Net current assets			52,450
Net assets			77,450
Financed by:			
Opening capital			85,000
Less: Net loss			4,350
Less: Drawings			3,200
Closing capital			77,450

REPORTING REGULATIONS FOR DIFFERENT TYPES OF ORGANISATIONS, THE LEGAL AND REGULATORY FRAMEWORK

24 USERS OF THE FINAL ACCOUNTS

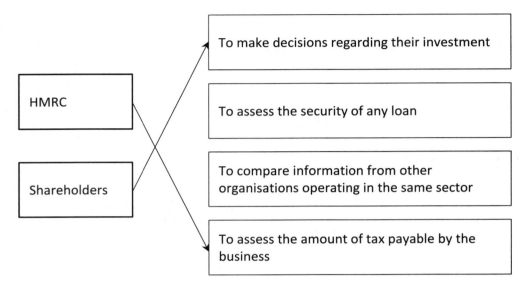

25 THE FQS

- Relevance

- Faithful representation.

26 BORIS

- **Going concern** is particularly relevant here because there is doubt over whether the business will continue trading for the foreseeable future.

27 CHARITIES

(a) The statement is **true**.

(b) The statement is **false**. A charitable purpose is one which is for the general benefit of the public.

28 INTERNATIONAL ACCOUNTING STANDARDS

IAS 2: Inventories should be valued at the lower of cost and net realisable value

IAS 16: Property, plant and equipment is measured at its cost and depreciated so that its depreciable amount is allocated over its useful economic life.

IAS 1: A complete set of financial statements must include a statement of profit or loss and a statement of financial position.

PARTNERSHIP ACCOUNTING

29 CELEBRATION CUPCAKES

Capital account – Erica

Goodwill	16,000	Balance b/d	10,000
Balance c/d	18,000	Goodwill	24,000
	34,000		34,000

30 WYN, FRANCIS AND BILL

(a) **Goodwill**

Capital – Wyn	27,000	Capital – Wyn	18,000
Capital – Francis	18,000	Capital – Francis	13,500
		Capital – Bill	13,500
	45,000		45,000

(b) **Capital account – Bill**

Goodwill	13,500	Bank	75,000
Balance c/d	61,500		
	75,000		75,000

31 FLORA, JASMINE AND MAVIS

(a)

Account name	Dr	Cr
Goodwill	£105,000	
Capital account – Flora		£36,750
Capital account – Jasmine		£68,250

(b) £31,750

New goodwill value = £105,000 + £22,000

= £127,000

× 25% = £31,750

32 PHIL, GEOFF AND JACK

(a) **Capital account – Jack**

Bank	31,000	Balance b/d	9,000
		Goodwill	15,000
		Current account	7,000
	31,000		31,000

(b) 2 The balance could be transferred to a Loan account.

33 DAN, KIM AND TED

Goodwill

Capital – Dan	40,000	Capital – Kim	50,000
Capital – Kim	30,000	Capital – Ted	50,000
Capital – Ted	30,000		
	100,000		100,000

34 RACHAEL, ED AND MATTY

Partnership appropriation account for the year ended 30 June 20X9

	£
Profit for the year	220,000
Salaries:	
Rachael	−18,000
Ed	0
Matty	−36,000
Interest on capital:	
Rachael	−2,000
Ed	−2,000
Matty	−2,000
Sales commission:	
Rachael	−8,250
Ed	−6,800
Matty	−4,715
Profit available for distribution	140,235

	£
Profit share:	
Rachael (40% × £140,235)	56,094
Ed (40% × £140,235)	56,094
Matty (20% × £140,235)	28,047
Total residual profit distributed	140,235

35 NYAH, SHAUNA AND MOLLIE

Partnership appropriation account for the year ended 31 March 20Y0

	£
Profit for the year	70,000
Salaries:	
Nyah	−25,000
Shauna	−19,000
Mollie	0
Sales commission	
Nyah	−1,100
Shauna	−1,100
Mollie	−1,100
Profit available for distribution	22,700

	£
Profit share:	
Nyah (35% × £22,700)	7,945
Shauna (20% × £22,700)	4,540
Mollie (45% × £22,700)	10,215
Total residual profit distributed	22,700

36   EDWARD, JAKE AND BELLA

Partnership appropriation account for the year ended 31 December 20X0

	£
Profit for the year	52,000
Salaries:	
Edward	−30,000
Jake	0
Bella	−21,000
Sales commission:	
Edward	−3,000
Jake	−3,000
Bella	−3,200
Interest on drawings:	
Edward	1,880
Jake	2,870
Bella	0
Residual profit/loss	−3,450

Profit/loss share:	
Edward (50% × −£3,450)	−1,725
Jake (20% × −£3,450)	−690
Bella (30% × −£3,450)	−1,035
Total residual profit / loss distributed	−3,450

37   GARY, MARK AND ROBBIE

Current accounts

	Gary £	Mark £	Robbie £		Gary £	Mark £	Robbie £
Drawings	34,000	30,000	58,000	Balance b/d	2,000	1,500	250
				Salaries	18,000	0	36,000
Balance c/d	23,000	6,500		Interest	5,000	3,000	3,750
				Profit share	32,000	32,000	16,000
				Balance c/d			2,000
	57,000	36,500	58,000		57,000	36,500	58,000

38   JOHN, JACKIE AND TEGAN

Current accounts

	John £	Jackie £	Tegan £		John £	Jackie £	Tegan £
Balance b/d	750			Balance b/d		1,900	600
Drawings	18,000	35,000	12,750	Salaries	11,000	16,500	0
Balance c/d	20,400	19,390	5,090	Interest	1,900	2,240	2,240
				Profit share	26,250	33,750	15,000
	39,150	54,390	17,840		39,150	54,390	17,840

39   LOUIS, CHERYL AND SIMON

Current accounts

	Louis £	Cheryl £	Simon £		Louis £	Cheryl £	Simon £
Drawings	25,000	10,200	31,000	Balance b/d	3,500	1,800	1,000
Balance c/d	39,500	4,600	9,400	Salaries	30,000	0	21,000
				Interest	1,000	1,000	400
				Profit share	30,000	12,000	18,000
	64,500	14,800	40,400		64,500	14,800	40,400

40   DEREK, JIN AND AHMED

Partnership Appropriation account for the year ended 31 March 20X8:

	£
Profit for the year	254,000
Salaries:	
Derek	−20,000
Jin	−24,000
Ahmed	0
Interest on capital:	
Derek	−8,000
Jin	−7,200
Ahmed	−10,560
Interest on drawings:	
Derek	4,600
Jin	3,800
Ahmed	4,800
Profit available for distribution	197,440

Profit share:	
Derek (3/10 × £197,440)	59,232
Jin (3/10 × £197,440)	59,232
Ahmed (4/10 × £197,440)	78,976
Total residual profit distributed	197,440

41   JACOB AND OLIVER

Partnership Appropriation account for the year ended 31 December 20X8:

	£
Profit for the year	182,225
Salaries:	
Jacob	–20,000
Oliver	–20,000
Interest on capital:	
Jacob	–2,800
Oliver	–6,250
Sales commission:	
Jacob	–1,560
Oliver	–2,690
Interest on drawings:	
Jacob	2,275
Oliver	0
Profit available for distribution	131,200

Profit share:	
Jacob (£131,200/2)	65,600
Oliver (£131,200/2)	65,600
Total residual profit distributed	131,200

PARTNERSHIP STATEMENT OF PROFIT OR LOSS

42   R & R TRADING

(a)

R & R Trading		
Statement of profit or loss for the year ended 30 September 20X7		
	£	£
Revenue (£173,050 – £2,200)		170,850
Opening inventory	17,700	
Purchases	98,000	
Closing inventory	–19,500	
Cost of goods sold		96,200
Gross profit		74,650
Less:		
Depreciation charge	7,100	
Discounts allowed	1,350	
General expenses	26,100	
Rent	7,300	
Wages	8,500	
Total expenses		50,350
Profit for the year		24,300

(b)

	£
Rita's share of the profit or loss (£24,300 × 55%)	13,365
Rita's final current account balance (£920 + £13,365 – £6,000)	8,285

43   OSMOND PARTNERSHIP

(a)

Osmond Partnership		
Statement of profit or loss for the year ended 31 March 20X1		
	£	£
Revenue (£164,000 – £1,500)		162,500
Opening inventory	3,450	
Purchases	125,000	
Closing inventory	–7,850	
Cost of goods sold		120,600
Gross profit		41,900
Add:		
Discounts received	900	
Disposal	450	
Total sundry income		1,350
Less:		
Depreciation charge	1,600	
Discounts allowed	345	
General expenses	2,950	
Rent	5,250	
Irrecoverable bad debt expense	295	
Wages	24,000	
Total expenses		34,440
Profit for the year		8,810

(b)

	£
Heather's share of the profit or loss (£8,810 × 50%)	4,405
Heather's final current account balance (–£400 + £4,405 – £3,250)	755

44 PERSEPHONE'S

(a)

Persephone's		
Statement of profit or loss for the year ended 30 June 20X8		
	£	£
Revenue		85,000
Opening inventory	9,100	
Purchases	38,700	
Closing inventory	−9,800	
Cost of goods sold		38,000
Gross profit		47,000
Plus:		
Allowance for doubtful debts adjustment		1,000
Less:		
Depreciation charge	800	
General expenses	8,200	
Rent	5,900	
Wages	8,500	
Total expenses		23,400
Profit for the year		24,600

(b)

	Tina (£)	Cher (£)	Total (£)
Current account Tina (W) £2,257 + (£24,600 × 60%) − £2,054 Cher (W) £3,750 + (£24,600 × 40%) − £2,553	14,963	11,037	26,000
Capital account (Trial balance figures)	2,050	2,050	4,100
	17,013	13,087	30,100

45   SUAREZ PARTNERSHIP

(a)

Suarez Partnership		
Statement of profit or loss for the year ended 30 June 20X6		
	£	£
Revenue		108,000
Opening inventory	13,100	
Purchases (£70,600 – £2,350)	68,250	
Closing inventory	–12,500	
Cost of goods sold		68,850
Gross profit		39,150
Plus:		
Profit on disposal		225
Less:		
Depreciation charge	925	
General expenses	9,300	
Rent	6,000	
Wages	12,000	
Total expenses		28,225
Profit for the year		11,150

(b)

	Louis (£)	Emilio (£)	Total (£)
Current account Louis (W) £1,500 + (£11,150 × 50%) – £2,500 Emilio (W) – £200 + (£11,150 × 50%) – £2,500	4,575	2,875	7,450
Capital account	4,160	3,000	7,160
	8,735	5,875	14,610

(c)
- The taxation charge for a limited company is shown as an expense in the statement of profit or loss. This statement is **true**.

- A limited company must prepare the final accounts every six months. This statement is **false**. Limited companies must prepare annual accounts.

- Only the carrying amount of each type of non-current asset is shown on the face of the statement of financial position. This statement is **true**. A breakdown of how the carrying amount has been calculated is shown in the notes to the accounts.

UNDERPINNING KNOWLEDGE

46 SHORT FORM QUESTIONS

1   (b)

2   (c)

3   (c)

4   (b)

5   (a)

6   (a)   A sole trader makes a credit sale (ignore sales tax)

	Debit	Credit	No change
Revenue		✓	
Loan			✓
Non-current assets			✓
Trade receivables	✓		

(b)   A sole trader decides to write off an irrecoverable debt

	Debit	Credit	No change
Trade payables			✓
Inventory			✓
Irrecoverable debt expense	✓		
Trade receivables		✓	

(c)   A sole trader purchases a new computer on credit for use in the business

	Debit	Credit	No change
Discount allowed			✓
Sundry payables		✓	
Non-current assets	✓		
Inventory			✓

(d)   A sole trader accounts for the cash received on disposal of a motor vehicle

	Debit	Credit	No change
Motor vehicles repairs			✓
Motor vehicles depreciation expense			✓
Disposal of motor vehicles account		✓	
Bank	✓		

(e)   A sole trader pays transport costs to have goods delivered to his premises

	Debit	Credit	No change
Bank		✓	
Carriage inwards	✓		
Carriage outwards			✓
Purchases			✓

(f)   A sole trader pays transport costs to have goods delivered to customers

	Debit	Credit	No change
Bank		✓	
Carriage inwards			✓
Carriage outwards	✓		
Sales			✓

Section 3

MOCK ASSESSMENT QUESTIONS

THIS ASSESSMENT CONSISTS OF SIX TASKS, WHICH ALL NEED TO BE COMPLETED.

THE STANDARD VAT RATE IS 20%.

TASK 1.1 (15 marks)

You are working on the accounts for a travel business for the year ended 31 October 20X8. There are no credit sales and you have the following additional information below:

Bank summary for the year ended 31 October 20X8

	£		£
Bal b/d	7,550	Rent	6,500
Cash sales (including VAT)	139,800	Payroll expenses	45,000
		Cash purchases (including VAT)	25,200
		Trade Payables	30,000
		Advertising	2,000
		Administration	4,800
		Light and heat	4,000
		HMRC for VAT	11,200
		Bal c/d	18,650
	147,350		**147,350**

Assets and liabilities at:	**31 October 20X7**	**31 October 20X8**
Closing inventory	2,500	1,500
VAT	17,150 credit	Not available
Trade payables	4,990	4,000

Notes:

- Goods totalling £624 (including VAT) which were originally purchased on credit were returned to payables during the year.

- The business took advantage of settlement discounts offered by suppliers of £270 (including VAT) during the year ended 31 October 20X8. The supplier sent a credit note for the discount which still needs to be recorded in the accounts.

(a) Calculate the sales excluding VAT for the year ended 31 October 20X8.

£_____ **(2 marks)**

(b) Identify the missing credit purchases figure by preparing the purchases ledger control account for the year ended 31 October 20X8. **(6 marks)**

	£		£
Total		Total	

(c) Calculate the closing balance on the VAT control account for the year ended 31 October 20X8.

Note the business is not charged VAT on its rent or any other expense where it has not been stated. **(7 marks)**

	£		£
Total		Total	

TASK 1.2 **(15 marks)**

You are given the following information about Minnie, a sole trader, as at 31 March 20X8:

The value of the assets and liabilities were

- Non-current assets at carrying amount £19,175
- Trade receivables £5,500
- Allowance for doubtful debts £350
- Inventory at 31 March 20X8 £6,755
- Prepayments £250
- Bank overdraft £575
- Trade payables £4,775
- Accruals £375
- Capital £19,000

There were no other assets or liabilities with the exception of part (a).

(a)   **Calculate the long term loan account balance as at 31 March 20X8.**

£_____

(2 marks)

(b)   On 1 June an item of equipment was disposed of and the proceeds were received in cash.

Tick the boxes to show what effect this transaction will have on the account balances. You must choose one answer for each line.   (5 marks)

Account name	Debit ✓	Credit ✓	No change ✓
Non-current assets at cost			
Accumulated depreciation			
Cash			
Payables			
Depreciation charge			

(c)   During the year ended 31 March 20X8 a business made sales of £90,000 and operates with a mark-up on cost of 20%. Inventory at 1 April 20X7 was £7,505.

Using this information and the information provided in part (a), complete the following tasks.   (5 marks)

(i)   **Calculate the cost of goods sold for the year ended 31 March 20X8.**

£_____

(ii)   **Calculate the cost of purchases.**

£_____

You are now working on the final accounts of JOR Partnership.

Your manager has been called away for an unexpected management meeting in London. He has asked you to calculate and record the depreciation for the above client, in his absence. You have never calculated depreciation before and you are unsure how to record it. Your manager requires the work to be completed by the end of the day.

(d)   **What should you do? Choose one of the following options:**   (3 marks)

- Call your mum to complete the task for you: she used to work in accounting.

- Explain the situation to your manager and ask if there is another person in the organisation who can help you.

- Call JOR Partnership and tell them that the deadline is going to be missed.

- Complete the task to the best of your ability.

TASK 1.3 (18 marks)

This task is about final accounts for sole traders.

During the year ended 31 March 20X8 a business made a profit of £20,000 and the proprietor also made drawings of £15,000. The capital balance at 31 March 20X8 was £45,000.

(a) **Calculate the capital of the business at 31 March 20X7.**

£_____ (2 marks)

You have the following trial balance for a sole trader known as Tanya Trading. All the necessary year-end adjustments have been made.

A profit of £54,550 for the year has been recorded.

Tanya Trading has a policy of showing trade receivables net of any allowance for doubtful debts.

Trial balance of Tanya Trading as at 30 June 20X8

	Dr £	Cr £
Capital		40,000
Drawings	15,000	
Fixtures and fittings – Cost	50,000	
Fixtures and fittings – Accumulated depreciation		27,600
Motor vehicle – Cost	10,000	
Motor vehicle – Accumulated depreciation		3,000
Closing inventory – Statement of financial position	3,480	
Closing inventory – Statement of profit or loss		3,480
Prepayments	890	
Accruals		1,000
Purchase ledger control account		6,000
Revenue		140,570
Bank	20,000	
Cash in hand	5,000	
Rent	7,200	
Payroll expenses	14,000	
Sales ledger control account	29,380	
Purchases	55,000	
Allowance for doubtful debts adjustment	220	
Allowance for doubtful debts		1,600
Advertising expenses	2,000	
Miscellaneous expenses	1,500	
Depreciation charge	6,600	
Opening inventory	2,980	
Total	**223,250**	**223,250**

(b) **Prepare a statement of financial position for the business as at 30 June 20X8.** **(16 marks)**

Statement of financial position of Tanya Trading as at 30 June 20X8.

	£	£	£
Non-current assets			
Current assets			
Current liabilities			
Net current assets			
Net assets			
Capital			

TASK 1.4 (16 marks)

(a) **Complete the following:** (10 marks)

(i) **Which of the following is an advantage of operating as a sole trader rather than a company? Choose one.**

- A sole trader has limited liability

- A sole trader never needs to prepare final accounts

- A sole trader can choose how the business is operated without consulting others

- A sole trader does not need to pay tax on their profits

(ii) **Who are the owners of a sole trader or partnership? Choose two of the following options:**

- The shareholders

- The partners

- The managers

- The sole trader

- The employees

- The trustees

(iii) **Complete the following statement about limited liability partnerships by choosing the correct option from the brackets.**

Limited liability partnerships (LLPs) are partnerships where (all of / some of / none of) the partners have limited liability. Limited liability is a type of (liability that does not exceed the amount invested in a partnership by a partner / liability that does exceed the amount invested in a partnership by a partner).

(b) **What is a Statement of Recommended Practice (SORP)? Choose one.** (2 marks)

- It's a document which provides guidance to charities on financial accounting and reporting

- It's a document which provides guidance to companies on financial accounting and reporting

- It's a document which provides guidance to sole traders on financial accounting and reporting

- It's a document which provides guidance to partnerships on financial accounting and reporting

(c) **Complete the following statement about the users of final accounts by choosing the correct option from the brackets.** (4 marks)

All users of financial statements are (internal / external / both internal and external) to the organisation. The reason shareholders use the financial statements is to (make decisions regarding their investment / to decide whether to apply for a job opportunity at the organisation / to compare information from other organisations operating within the same business sector). Banks are interested in the financial statements to (make a decision regarding their personal investment / assess the ability of the business to pay interest and repay loans / assess whether the organisation should change banks).

TASK 1.5 (15 marks)

Evan, Charles and Roanne have been in partnership for many years.

On 30 June 20X7, Evan retired from the partnership when the goodwill of the business was valued at £36,000. The goodwill has not yet been accounted for.

The profit sharing ratio effective until 30 June 20X7 was 4:3:3 with Evan taking the larger share. Charles and Roanne shared profits and losses equally from 1 July 20X7.

Goodwill should be introduced into the accounts on 30 June 20X7 and then immediately eliminated.

(a) **Show the entries required to introduce the goodwill into the accounts at 30 June 20X7.**

(5 marks)

Account name	Amount £	Debit	Credit

Options for account name: Goodwill / Current account – Evan / Current account – Charles / Current account – Roanne / Capital account – Evan / Capital account – Charles / Capital account – Roanne / Bank / Salaries.

You have the following information about another partnership known as the Simpson partnership for the year ended 30 June 20X8. The partners are Peter and Simon.

All the year-end adjustments have been made, except for the transfer of profit to current accounts of the partners.

The partnership agreement allows for the following:

- Partners' annual salaries

    – Peter £25,000

    – Simon £10,000

- Sales commission earned during the year

    – Peter £786

    – Simon £1,134

- Profit share

    – Peter 1/3

    – Simon 2/3

- During the year Peter made £18,000 of drawings and Simon £22,000.

- Profit available for distribution was £126,060.

(b) Update the partners' current accounts for the partnership for the year ended 30 June 20X8, showing the balances carried down. **(8 marks)**

	Peter £	Simon £		Peter £	Simon £
Balance b/d	15,000	11,000			

(c) Which of the following is included in the final accounts for a partnership? Choose one of the following options: **(2 marks)**

- Partnership current account bank statement

- Percentage of which sales commission is allowed per partner

- Partnership statement of profit or loss

- Partnership Act 1890

TASK 1.6   (21 marks)

You have been provided with the following trial balance for Egan partnership.

The partners are Taylah and Ella. They share profits and losses in the ratio 60:40 with Taylah taking the larger share.

Egan partnership Trial Balance as at 30 June 20X8	Dr £	Cr £
Sales		789,082
Purchases	373,593	
Opening inventory	41,211	
Payroll expenses	161,326	
General expenses	72,900	
Motor expenses	14,633	
Allowance for doubtful debts adjustment		750
Allowance for doubtful debts		2,675
Motor vehicles – Cost	37,400	
Accumulated depreciation – MV		19,160
Fixtures and fittings – Cost	46,100	
Accumulated depreciation – F&F		20,855
Capital account – Taylah		26,200
Capital account – Ella		37,800
Current account – Taylah	15,000	
Current account – Ella	11,000	

Egan partnership Trial Balance as at 30 June 20X8	Dr £	Cr £
Drawings – Taylah	18,000	
Drawings – Ella	22,000	
Sales ledger control account	70,367	
Purchase ledger control account		25,682
Bank	26,338	
VAT		4,529
Closing inventory	54,426	54,426
Disposal	3,870	
Depreciation charge	12,995	
	981,159	981,159

(a) **Using this information, prepare a statement of profit or loss for the Egan partnership for the year ended 30 June 20X8. The only values to be shown as negatives should be a deduction from cost of sales and, if applicable, a net loss for the year.** **(15 marks)**

Statement of profit or loss for Egan partnership for the year ended 30 June 20X8.

	£	£
Revenue		
Cost of sales		
Gross profit		
Sundry income		
Expenses		
Total expenses		
Profit/(loss) for the year		

(b) **(i)** Calculate Ella's share of the profit or loss and her final current account balance, use the table provided below. **(4 marks)**

	£
Ella's share of the profit or loss	
Ella's final current account balance	

(ii) Where will the VAT balance appear in the statement of financial position? Choose one of the following options:

- As a non-current asset
- As a current asset
- As a current liability
- Within the 'Financed by' section

Preparation of limited company accounts differs from the preparation of sole trader and partnership accounts.

(c) **Notes to the accounts only need to be prepared for the managers of the company.**

TRUE / FALSE **(2 marks)**

Section 4

MOCK ASSESSMENT ANSWERS

TASK 1.1

(a) **£116,500** (£139,800 × 100/120)

(b) **Purchases ledger control account**

	£		£
Payments to payables	30,000	Balance b/d	4,990
Discount received	270	**Credit purchases (bal)**	**29,904**
Purchase returns	624		
Balance c/d	4,000		
Total	**34,894**	**Total**	**34,894**

(c) **Sales tax control**

	£		£
Cash purchases (£25,200 × 20/120)	4,200	Balance b/d	17,150
HMRC	11,200	Cash sales (£139,800 × 20/120)	23,300
Credit purchases (£29,904 × 20/120)	4,984	Purchase returns (£624 × 20/120)	104
Balance c/d	20,215	PLCA (VAT on discount received)	45
Total	**40,599**	**Total**	**40,599**

TASK 1.2

(a)   **£6,605** (£19,175 + £5,500 − £350 + £6,755 + £250 − £575 − £4,775 − £375 − £19,000)

(b)

Account name	Debit ✓	Credit ✓	No change ✓
Non-current assets at cost		✓	
Accumulated depreciation	✓		
Cash	✓		
Payables			✓
Depreciation charge			✓

(c)   (i)   **£75,000** (£90,000 / 120 × 100)

      (ii)   **£74,250** (£75,000 + £6,755 − £7,505)

(d)   Explain the situation to your manager and ask if there is another person in the organisation who can help you.

TASK 1.3

(a)   **£40,000** (£45,000 − £20,000 + £15,000)

(b)   **Statement of financial position of Tanya Trading as at 30 June 20X8.**

	£	£	£
Non-current assets			
Fixtures and fittings	50,000	27,600	22,400
Motor vehicles	10,000	3,000	7,000
	60,000	30,600	**29,400**
Current assets			
Inventory		3,480	
Receivables (£29,380 − £1,600)		27,780	
Prepayments		890	
Bank		20,000	
Cash in hand		5,000	
		57,150	
Current liabilities			
Accruals	1,000		
Payables	6,000		
		7,000	

	£	£	£
Net current assets			**50,150**
Net assets			**79,550**
Capital			
Opening capital			40,000
Add: Profit for the year			54,550
Less: Drawings			15,000
Closing capital			**79,550**

TASK 1.4

(a) (i) A sole trader can choose how the business is operated without consulting others.

(ii) The partners

The sole trader

(iii) Limited liability partnerships (LLPs) are partnerships where **some of** the partners have limited liability. Limited liability is a type of **liability that does not exceed the amount invested in a partnership by a partner**.

(b) It's a document which provides guidance to charities on financial accounting and reporting.

(c) All users of financial statements are **both internal and external** to the organisation. The reason shareholders use the financial statements is to **make decisions regarding their investment**. Banks are interested in the financial statements to **assess the ability of the business to pay interest and repay loans**.

TASK 1.5

(a)

Account name	Amount £	Debit	Credit
Goodwill	36,000	X	
Capital account – Evan (4/10 × £36,000)	14,400		X
Capital account – Charles (3/10 × £36,000)	10,800		X
Capital account – Roanne (3/10 × £36,000)	10,800		X

(b) **Current accounts**

	Peter £	Simon £		Peter £	Simon £
Balance b/d	15,000	11,000	Salaries	25,000	10,000
Drawings	18,000	22,000	Sales commission	786	1,134
Balance c/d	34,806	62,174	Profit share	42,020	84,040
	67,806	95,174		67,806	95,174

(c) Partnership statement of profit or loss.

TASK 1.6

(a)   **Statement of profit or loss for Egan partnership for the year ended 30 June 20X8**

	£	£
Revenue		789,082
Cost of sales		
Opening inventory	41,211	
Purchases	373,593	
Closing inventory	(54,426)	
		360,378
Gross profit		428,704
Sundry income		
Allowance for doubtful debts adjustment		750
Expenses		
Payroll expenses	161,326	
General expenses	72,900	
Motor expenses	14,633	
Disposal	3,870	
Depreciation charge	12,995	
Total expenses		265,724
Profit/(loss) for the year		163,730

(b)   (i)

	£
Ella's share of the profit or loss (£163,730 × 40%)	65,492
Ella's final current account balance (−£11,000 − £22,000 + £65,492)	32,492

(ii)   As a current liability.

(c)   FALSE